DERBY

NORTHE

WALKS FOR MOTORISTS

Clifford Thompson

30 Walks with sketch maps

COUNTRYSIDE BOOKS
NEWBURY, BERKSHIRE

Countryside Books' walking guides cover most areas of England and Wales and include the following series:

County Rambles
Walks For Motorists
Exploring Long Distance Paths
Literary Walks

A complete list is available from the publishers

First published 1981
by Frederick Warne Ltd.

This completely revised and updated edition published 1992

COUNTRYSIDE BOOKS
3 Catherine Road
Newbury, Berkshire

ISBN 1 85306 167 0

Cover photograph of Upperdale
taken by the Author.

Publishers' Note

At the time of publication all footpaths used in these walks were designated as official footpaths or rights of way, but it should be borne in mind that diversion orders may be made from time to time.

Although every care has been taken in the preparation of this Guide, neither the Author nor the Publisher can accept responsibility for those who stray from the Rights of Way.

Typeset by Acorn Bookwork, Salisbury, Wiltshire
Produced through MRM Associates Ltd., Reading
Printed in England by J.W. Arrowsmith Ltd., Bristol

Contents

DERBYSHIRE
Northern Area

Numbers show where the walks begin

Introduction

North Derbyshire is a surprisingly rural area. There is industry, but it is mainly centred around Chesterfield. There are large mineral workings, in particular north and south of Buxton. More to the centre of the area the quarries are more discreet and do not impose themselves as much on the visitor. To the north are the peat moors of the dark peak. In the centre are the gritstone edges. Elsewhere are the fields, the dales and the wood. The walks in this book reflect this diversity.

It is hardly surprising that the northernmost part of Derbyshire attracts so many visitors. Because of access agreements with landowners, particularly the Duke of Devonshire, walkers can, for most of the year, wander at will over most of the moorland with a freedom denied in rural and agricultural areas. There is a challenge, a remoteness, a magnetic desolation on the heights of the northern moors that is not found elsewhere in the county. Walks 1–3 explore this landscape.

As with other similar regions there are several mountain rescue centres in the area backed up by volunteer teams who are prepared, day and night, to come to the aid of anybody in difficulties. To avoid having to call on their help, remember the following hints for hill walkers.

Be sure to have strong footwear that grips. Protective and spare warm clothing are essential for all hill walking. For the more wild and pathless regions always take a map and compass, reserve food and first aid kit. Think twice before going alone. Leave word of your intended route. Be sure of sufficient daylight. Take no risks with the weather – it can be as severe at 2,000 feet as at 20,000 feet.

North Derbyshire is rich in the remains of all eras. The many mystic stone circles and prehistoric relics indicate the intensity of early life. The Romans were more interested in the commercial aspect of Derbyshire and the scars remain where easily obtainable lead was removed from the earth.

The Romans left, and other nationalities had passing

interests and left their mark. The Danish influence is greatly in evidence, and they were followed by the Normans. Later, grand houses were built and then the railways came to alter the face of the land. Richard Arkwright, whose development in spinning technique led to wholesale changes in the cotton industry, was known in the area. The Derbyshire edges once resounded to the sound of hammer on chisel to produce, for a time at least, their world famous millstones.

Walks 4–11 provide a miniature of Derbyshire's past which may tempt the reader and the walker to more serious investigation.

The few hills in the county that just top 2,000 feet are all to the north of Edale. Within sight of Castleton are a few mountains, with Mam Tor the highest at 1,700 feet.

One important point about a mountain is not particularly that it is there, but that when you get there you can see where you have come from; and beyond. The hills climbed in this section all have that distinction. You can see a long way when you get there. Also there are good footpaths to help you reach the summits. Walks 12–15 scale these heights.

Walks 16–19 explore the county's beautiful reservoirs. There are very few reservoirs in Derbyshire south of the Hope Valley and there is a good reason for that. The ground simply cannot cope with the water. Limestone has many qualities, but water retention is not one of them. As a great deal of the land south of the Hope Valley is limestone based, water must be stored in other places.

Offsetting this, to the north of the Hope Valley the under-lying rock is millstone grit, shale and shale grit, good bases for reservoirs. There are deep valleys and rain falls in greater quantity there then further south.

The reservoirs of Longdendale and Derwent Dale serve a wide area and there are others to the east and west. The Goyt Valley, with its two reservoirs, one a yachting reservoir, is a noted beauty spot. Linacre Reservoirs have their beauty and also fish; consequently they too are popular.

A Derbyshire dale is different from a Yorkshire dale in more than one respect. Wharfedale or Wensleydale, for instance, are called by their respective names for many miles and keep their names until the dale ends. Not always so in Derbyshire. In the course of only a few miles the valley with the river Dove flowing through it has three names – Beresford Dale, Wolfscote Dale and Dove Dale. The intermittent valley from Peak Forest to Miller's Dale changes its name whenever it is crossed by a road, hence Dam Dale, Hay Dale, Peter Dale and Monk's Dale.

The average Derbyshire dale is narrow and partially wooded, with rolling hillsides. Some, like Dove Dale and Lathkill Dale, are thickly wooded with sparkling rivers. All are worth exploring.

Walks 20–27 provide a cross section of the Derbyshire dales. Elsewhere in the book are other dales. If there is a valley there is a dale and if there is a dale there is a name.

Finally, walks 28–30 are about villages, some large, but mainly small, and all having their own unique character.

The countryside would be lifeless without its villages. They are an essential part of our heritage and never more so than in North Derbyshire where the land is tied together by small communities, where people have lived, sometimes, for centuries.

About half of north Derbyshire is part of the Peak District National Park whose administrative offices are at Bakewell. They have permanent information centres at Buxton, Edale, Castleton and Bakewell, besides mobile units. Each year a programme of Peak Park events is published and is available at the centres. It is always worth checking to see what is on before having a day out in order to combine a walk with, say, a 'well dressing'.

A sketch map is provided with each walk, but it is best to use the relevant Ordnance Survey map as well. These are the 1:50,000 series:

No. 110 Sheffield and Huddersfield

No. 119 Buxton, Matlock and Dovedale
No. 120 Mansfield and the Dukeries.

Better still are the Ordnance Survey Outdoor Leisure maps, Dark Peak area and White Peak area to a scale of 1:25,000. Most walks are covered by these maps. With every walk the relevant maps are listed.

Throughout the book grid references are given to locate the starting place of each walk. These are taken from the relevant Ordnance Survey map, and for anyone not familiar with the grid system, a study of the explanatory notes on any Ordnance Survey map is useful.

Finally, how to behave when out walking is largely common sense, but it is always a good idea to remember the Country Code.

Clifford Thompson
Spring 1992

The Country Code

Guard against fire risk.
Fasten all gates.
Keep dogs under proper control.
Keep to paths across farmland.
Avoid damaging fences, hedges and walls.
Leave no litter.
Safeguard water supplies.
Protect wildlife, wild plants and trees.
Go carefully on country roads.
Respect the life of the countryside.

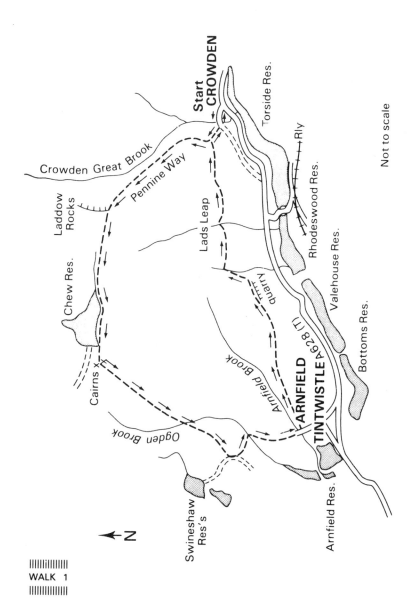

Start CROWDEN

Crowden Great Brook

Pennine Way

Laddow Rocks

Chew Res.

Cairns x

Ogden Brook

Swineshaw Res's

Lads Leap

quarry

Arnfield Brook

ARNFIELD

TINTWISTLE A628 (T)

Arnfield Res.

Torside Res.

Rly

Rhodeswood Res.

Valehouse Res.

Bottoms Res.

Not to scale

N

WALK 1

CHEW RESERVOIR

WALK 1

★

12 miles (19.5 km)

OS Landranger 110, Dark Peak

Summer Saturday evenings see many tents near Crowden Youth Hostel and many are the overnight visitors at the hostel itself. This will have been their first day along the Pennine Way. The next day will be spent walking up to Laddow Rocks, on to the peat moor of Black Hill and on over the morass of White Moss. You may well walk with these Pennine Way walkers, but only as far as Laddow Rocks.

The walk starts at Crowden car park (SK 074 993), just off the A628.

Take the exit to the toilets and turn right at the toilets to walk past the camp site reception area to turn left on the gated water works road. After a short climb turn right at the Pennine Way sign to take the path gradually climbing the hill. After an initial ascent the path descends a little and Laddow Rocks can be seen in the distance. Sometimes climbers can be seen clinging to the high rock face. After a short descent the path returns to an ascent and eventually reaches the rocks.

Take the prominent cairn-strewn path that leaves the rocks and very soon Chew Reservoir comes into view and is passed. At the reservoir foot proceed forward across a short stretch of moorland to the path on the high valley edge. From here can be seen Dove Stone Reservoir, a yachting lake. After about ¾ mile turn left at two prominent cairns and leave the edge walk. Follow cairns and posts over the moors and descend to Ogden Brook. Cross the stream at the sign 'Footpath to Arnfield and

11

Banks' and continue on a cairned and staked path, gradually descending to walled fields and power lines with massive pylons.

When the path meets a track at the sign 'Footpath to Chew Valley' turn left down the track. This is just before enclosed land and power lines. Follow the track across a stream and up the bank beyond and at the left bend climb a stile in the wall corner next to a pylon and take the field path passing to the right of the pylon. This gradually descends to a farm nestling in the valley ahead. Take the road around the right hand side of the farm and just before the second farm, after crossing a stream, turn left on to a grassed track at the sign 'Footpath to open country'.

This is now a gradual climb up the hillside which is used by shooting parties, as the butts further along will indicate. There is no danger, however, as this is a public footpath and on shooting days there are wardens to notify walkers. Occasional stakes confirm the path, although this is quite plain. Before a steep part in the path a pipe can be seen to the right, and shortly afterwards the reservoirs in Longdendale come into view. High across the valley is Bleaklow. At this point a fence is reached and for some distance the path is alongside the fence. When the path has passed the top side of an old quarry and two stiles over the fence are reached, turn left up the hillside at the sign 'To Arnfield, to Crowden' and take the path towards a post in the middle distance. After this head for the post on the skyline. Climbing is now completed.

Turn right and walk along the edge and when the path crosses a stream at the top of a steep ravine follow cairns and posts gradually descending, then steeply descending to rejoin the Pennine Way to retrace your steps to Crowden.

DERWENT

WALK 2

★

6 miles (9.5 km)

OS Landranger 110, Dark Peak

Derwent Reservoir was built in 1916 to add to Howden Reservoir completed four years earlier to increase water supplies to Sheffield, Derby, Nottingham and Leicester. For many people the reservoir will bring back memories of the Dam Busters raid and subsequent film because it was used as a training lake for the raid. The walk is alongside the reservoir and the return a pleasant moorland walk high above the water.

The walk starts from Fairholmes car park (SK 173 893).

Take the footpath close to the information centre to join the road that goes from one side of the valley to the other. When the road turns right take a footpath on the left of the road to ascend to the right side of the dam wall dominating the valley. The path joins the reservoir road just above the dam wall.

Walk north along the reservoir road almost as far as Howden Reservoir. Look out for a track to the right and 10 yards along it turn right across the grass to join a path rising through the trees. Beyond the plantation wall continue in the same direction on a path by a gulley.

When a sign is reached follow the Strines sign following a wall on your right. Near a ruined building continue on the path that now leaves the wall. Its continuation can be seen in the distance rising to the skyline. It is about here that the Strines path leaves your path at a signpost, to climb directly up the hill.

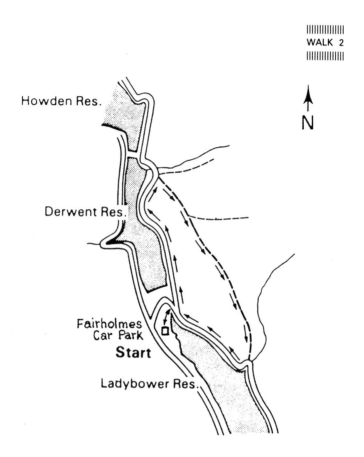

Howden Res.

N

Derwent Res.

Fairholmes
Car Park
Start

Ladybower Res.

Not to scale

14

When the skyline is reached at a ladder stile follow the path across the moors. It is about here that small footpath signs appear and are to be seen until the descent from the moors is made. From the ladder stile the path crosses the moor well to the right of a small plantation. Over to the right can be seen another path. This is not in your route. Having passed the trees the path follows a wall. At the wall corner turn left and descend to the left of a tip to pass through a gate to join a more distinct track. On reaching a farm take a gate to the left and continue descending in the gulley beyond to the reservoir road. Walk in a north easterly direction and return to Fairholmes.

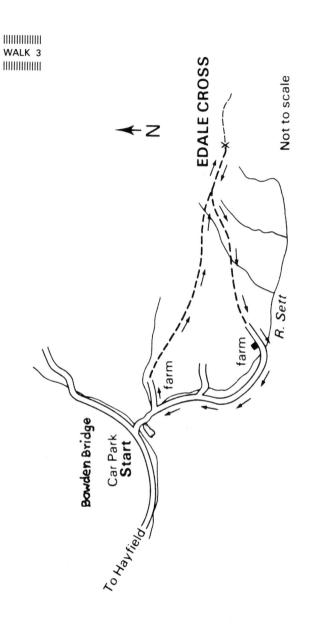

WALK 3

EDALE CROSS

N

Not to scale

Bowden Bridge

Car Park
Start

To Hayfield

farm

farm

R. Sett

EDALE CROSS

WALK 3

★

5 miles (8 km)

OS Landranger 110, Dark Peak

This walk hardly goes on to the heights of Kinder Scout, but the hills are always there overshadowing the walk.

Edale Cross itself may not be as old as it looks, dating back perhaps to 1610, but it is a landmark on the old pack horse track from Hayfield to Edale.

The walk starts from Bowden Bridge car park (SK 049 870) on the road to Kinder Reservoir from Hayfield.

Cross the road and bridge to take the road that runs parallel at first to the one that led to the car park. Nearby is Hayfield camp site and next to the road is a pond barred to casual visitors. Keep to the road following a stream until the drive to Tunstead House is reached. Take the track climbing directly up the hill.

When the track turns sharp right towards a farm take the path passing to the right of the farm buildings and then resume the climb up the hill first of all on a track then on a path up the fields. After passing through one gate turn right and follow the path that now obliquely climbs the hill on a more gentle ascent. A signpost will indicate the way. Over to the right are the peaks of South Head and Mount Famine.

Continue on a well-defined path, continually rising until a more prominent track is joined rising from the valley bottom. Keep to the track to ascend to Edale Cross. This is at the top of the hill. Beyond, the old pack horse road descends via Jacob's Ladder to the Vale of Edale. To the left a path climbs

17

to the rocks above. This is part of the alternative Pennine Way route over Kinder Scout recommended during bad weather.

Retrace your steps down the old trail, but instead of turning right on the path originally climbed continue down the trail that becomes a metalled road before reaching a farm. Continue on the road that turns right at the bottom of the hill and after crossing a stream ascends a little, but eventually descends down the valley back to the car park.

STANTON MOOR

WALK 4

★

2½ miles (4 km)

OS Landranger 119, White Peak

Stanton Moor is a magical place: here is prehistory. Besides various tumuli there is a small circle of nine stones called Nine Ladies, and near it King's Stone, both with low walls surrounding them. On the eastern edge is a square tower commemorating the passing of the Reform Bill in 1832. There are several prominent stones including the Cork Stone and Heart Stone. On the western side are acres of overgrown quarries although the stone industry in the district is by no means dead, as witness Twyfords at nearby Birchover. Besides all this there are excellent views in most directions, for this is a high plateau.

This short walk starts at a stone-barricaded entrance to the moor just under ½ mile north of the T junction above Birchover (SK 242 628) and about ¼ mile beyond Anne Twyford Dimensional Stone Ltd.

Pass on to the moor beyond the stone barricade and the stile beyond and walk through the trees to the first prominent stone. This is the Cork Stone and has small rungs up one side. Turn left at the stone then left at the next fork to follow the path that meanders across the moor passing numerous old quarries on your left. When a track is reached turn right, but after a few yards at a fork take the left turn to visit the tower visible over the trees.

After visiting the tower retrace your steps to the track and take the other branch of the fork. A few yards along and off

19

the track to the right are the Nine Ladies and beyond them the King's Stone.

Continue along the track and when another track is met turn right. Before continuing, another stone, the Heart Stone, is over to the left. Walk on the track passing the Cork Stone and return to the start.

HARTHILL MOOR

WALK 5

★

3½ miles (5.5 km)

OS Landranger 119, White Peak

Whether Robin Hood actually did stride around this area is open to doubt, but his name has been given to a cluster of rocks in an area noted for its historic connections. Nearby is a hermit's cave, a shallow affair now enclosed in railings. A little further away is a stone circle, the Ninestones, four standing stones remaining from the original nine. Near Harthill Moor Farm is an old fortification, a raised mound with a ditch.

Elton is the starting place (SK 222 610), an attractive Derbyshire village not far from Winster. The walk begins at All Saints' church.

Walk down Well Street, opposite The Duke of York and next to the church, then take the track on the left at the sign 'Public Footpath to Youlgreave'. Just along the track pass into a field turning left and then right to walk down the right hand side of a high hedge. At the bottom of the field pass through a stile and, bearing slightly right, walk on the path faintly seen climbing the hill via stiles to join a road at the sign 'Public Footpath, Elton ½'.

Cross the road to the stile opposite and signed 'Public Footpath, Youlgreave 2'. Climb the field ahead and after the next stile walk along the wall side. After the next stile walk diagonally across a field to a stile and on to a farm road. The farm itself is 100 yards to the left.

Cross the track and walk along the wall side, and beyond a stile head for a wood two field lengths away. Walk round

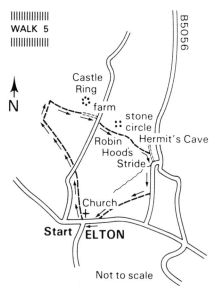

N

Castle Ring

farm

stone circle

Robin Hood's Stride

Hermit's Cave

Church

Start ELTON

B5056

Not to scale

the left side of the wood which is composed of all manner of trees, deciduous and evergreen. After crossing the next stile follow the power lines to another stile. Cross the next field and over a wall just to the right of a power pylon. Walk with a wall to your right as far as a gateway. Just beyond the gateway turn right through a gate, then a stile, to climb the hill diagonally, aiming halfway between two groups of trees on the skyline until a stile is taken about 50 yards from the top of the field.

At the very top, inside the farm, is the mound of an old fort. All that remains is the mound where the wall is, but below the wall is a ditch which would have been a defence for the fort.

After crossing the stile, cross the next field to a small gate near the wall corner, turn left, walk round the farm to the farm road and walk to the road ahead.

Cross the road and take the path signposted 'Footpath' towards a mass of rocks. This is Robin Hood's Stride. At the signpost, to the left, can be seen the stone circle, Ninestones, in another field. The path joins a track to the left of the rocks and descends to a farm road below.

The hermit's cave can be reached from the top of the track over to the left beyond a small wood and below another mass of rocks underneath a towering cliff of rock.

At the farm road turn right and walk to the road at the bottom. Across from the road gate take a narrow road which runs parallel to the metalled road for a little way then gradually climbs. When well past a house with '1737' engraved above the door, turn right over a stile at the sign 'Public Footpath, Elton ½' to climb diagon-ally up the hill to a stile next to a dead tree. Beyond this climb a hill to more power lines. Follow the fence above and, just beyond Elton Cricket Ground, turn left along a track to rejoin Elton at the eastern end of the village.

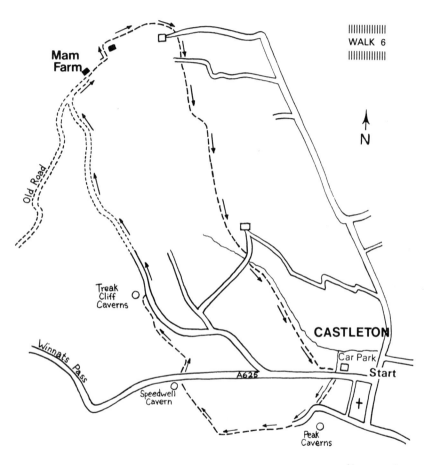

WALK 6

N

Mam Farm

Old Road

Treak Cliff Caverns

Winnats Pass

Speedwell Cavern

A625

CASTLETON

Car Park

Start

Peak Caverns

Not to scale

CASTLETON

WALK 6

4 miles (6.5 km)

OS Landranger 110, Dark Peak

William Peveril, an adventuring son of William the Conqueror, built Peveril Castle using stone taken from the old Roman fort at Brough further down the Hope valley. This castle ruin dominates the village and is one of several historical features in this area. Castleton attracts thousands of visitors and is particularly attractive in December when the Christmas decorations adorn the shops and streets.

The walk starts at Castleton car park (SK 149 830) and visits a few historical locations.

Leave the car park, crossing the road to take the riverside walk to Peak Caverns, as directed by a signpost. This takes you through some of the most attractive parts of Castleton. After reaching the river bridge close to the Peak Caverns, continue on the road climbing Goosehill, which continues as a narrow track beyond the road end, bearing gradually right and at a gate enters open country. The path taken beyond the gate gradually bears right alongside a wall to reach the Winnats Pass road just below Speedwell Caverns which can be seen when entering the field above Goosehill.

Cross the road and stile at the other side of the road into a field. Cross the field and over the stile in the wall ahead to skirt a small wood and walk on the path to Treak Cliff Caverns seen ahead. At the concrete drive and steps to the hillside caverns descend and turn left on the road at the bottom of the steps. This is the road that was the Castleton–

Chapel-on-le-Frith road before a disastrous land slip some years ago blocked and overran the road. As you walk up the road you will see plenty of evidence of its effects.

When the road officially stops at a turning circle there are two points of historical interest. To the left is the Odin Mine where minerals such as blue john and malachite can be found, but not taken.

Seen below on the right is a metal ring and attendant mill stone where years ago minerals were crushed.

Continue walking up the old road through a series of bends and at a pronounced sharp left bend leave the road at a footpath sign down the Mam Farm road. Bypass the farm and ahead at Mam Farm Cottage climb the hill to the left as indicated to bypass the buildings, crossing a field and following a path contouring the hill eventually to drop on to the track approaching the next farm.

Cross the farm road and over a way-marked stile to descend a field to the left of a fence, then a shallow depression, then a fence, with yellow markers along the way. The path crosses a stream at a footpath sign and continues on the right hand side of the stream. When a farm road is reached, which crosses another stream, continue along the fence side to your left crossing fields until the edge of Castleton is reached. A wall apparently bars all further progress, but there is a stile in the right hand corner and the path beyond leads to the road leading into Castleton. Turn left and return to the car park.

PEAK FOREST

WALK 7

★

4 miles (6.5 km)

OS Landranger 110 and 119, Dark Peak and White Peak

The village of Peak Forest was once the Gretna Green of Derbyshire. Romantic marriages took place here, often after long, moorland chases, until the Fleet Street Marriage Act changed it all in 1753. Peak Forest lies almost under the shadow of Eldon Hill, which is gradually being sliced up by Eldon Hill Quarries for its limestone.

The walk starts at Old Dam (SK 116 797), the hamlet next to Peak Forest.

Take the narrow road heading east marked as a cul-de-sac and after ¼ mile turn left along a track leading to a farm and a wood. When the track forks at the farm gate take the right turn into the wood and follow it as far as it goes.

This is Oxlow Rake, another long-abandoned lead mining working. In fact for most of the walk there are numerous small, grass covered humps and hollows where once men hewed with pick and shovel. The track gradually ascends through the trees and reverts to grass beyond the trees in a field to eventually join a lane at a stile. Turn left and when the track turns sharp right at a public bridleway sign proceed forward on the grass track alongside a wall on your left.

When a gate crosses the track pass through the gate on to the walled track ahead until a field on the left is reached with a motorcycle scrambling track. This is an earth track curling around the hillside. Ahead can be seen the workings of Eldon Hill Quarries.

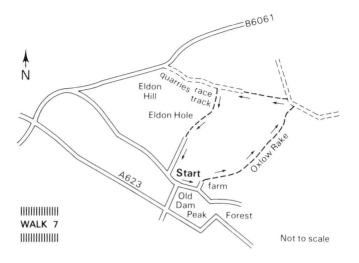

WALK 7

Turn into the field with the race track, walking alongside the wall to the left. At a wire fence negotiate a gate and take the grass track beyond as it rounds the hill. Keep on the track as it gradually descends the hill never far from the wall on the left.

As the hill is descended and before a stile is reached, over to the right can be seen Eldon Hole, one of only two Derbyshire pot holes. Just below the hill is a wood and just to the right is Eldon Hole, looking like a depression in the ground. This was once thought to be bottomless, but is actually 200 ft deep with further entrances to lower caverns.

Eventually, at a gate and stile, the way becomes a walled track and lower down at a farm a metalled road descending directly to Old Dam.

THE MAGPIE MINE

WALK 8

★

7 miles (11 km)

OS Landranger 119, White Peak

Lead mining used to be one of the major industries in Derbyshire. The Romans were probably the first to dig out the metal on a commercial basis, but they were followed over the centuries by others who could see large fortunes easily amassed by digging the stuff from the ground. Unfortunately for many of them, water proved too big a problem and a lot of mines had to be abandoned as it was costing more to remove the water than the lead.

The Magpie Mine survives as one of the better preserved lead mines in Derbyshire and is now the headquarters of the Peak District Mines Historical Society.

The walk starts at the church at Ashford-in-the-Water (SK 195 697).

Walk towards the octagonal shelter near the Riverside Hotel and cross the river by the sheepwash bridge to the A6. Turn right and walk along the road and turn left along the Sheldon road. About 100 yards along the narrow road on the left is an overgrown, tree-covered quarry. What looks like shale or dirty slate is Ashford black marble. This can easily be polished to give a high, black gloss which was greatly prized in Victorian times for its ornamental value. A little further along the road, but across the river, was the mill where the marble was worked.

Further along the Sheldon road turn right, at a public footpath sign, into a field to take the riverside path. An old

29

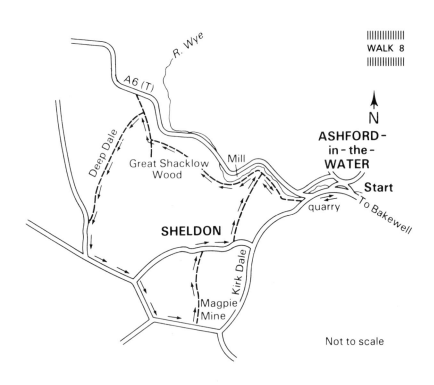

N

ASHFORD -
in - the -
WATER

Start

To Bakewell

quarry

R. Wye

A6 (T)

Deep Dale

Great Shacklow
Wood

Mill

SHELDON

Kirk Dale

Magpie
Mine

Not to scale

mill with water wheels is reached near a bridge over the river. Go round the left side of the mill into Great Shacklow Wood. Follow the path that soon leaves the river and ascend gradually through the trees continuing until a stile and footpath sign is met. Turn right and descend by the path. A left turn would take you directly to Sheldon. Lower down can be seen the A6 where is to be found a public car park.

Towards the bottom of the valley look for a low signpost and veer left as directed by 'Bridleway to Deep Dale'. This dale is soon reached and entered. Follow the path to climb the valley with a wall to your right. This is a dry valley, in part wooded, leading directly away from the main road. Towards the top of the dale pass through a gate at a 'Public Bridleway' sign and continue onwards now with the wall to your left, eventually to enter a track. Turn left and walk to the road ahead. Again turn left along the road. Straight ahead are the buildings of Magpie Mine.

Walk along the road and turn left up the track leading to the old mine.

From the mill chimney walk away from the mill and take the stile in the far left corner of the field. Cross the next field towards farm buildings. At a short walled track bear right and head for Sheldon church now visible. At the road running through the village turn right and descend to the bend in the road. Just round the bend at a farm turn left through a stile at the 'Public Footpath to Ashford' sign and follow the path down the bottom of the valley. A thick wood is soon entered at a stile. At the bottom of the valley rejoin the riverside path and return to Ashford.

N

To Sheffield

Redmires Res's

Not to scale

A57

To Strines

Moscar Lodge

Start

Stanage Edge

Stanage Pole

Roman Road

WALK 9

STANAGE EDGE

WALK 9

★

9 miles (14.5 km)

OS Landranger 110, Dark Peak

Two hundred years ago there was a thriving industry on the Derbyshire edges, Stanage Edge in particular, probably because it is longer than the others, stretching for four miles south of the Sheffield–Glossop A57 road. Millstones were cut at the 'edges' and sold. Sadly, imported French stones were cheaper and of finer quality and local industry died. Unfinished or unsold stones were abandoned and the edge has since been taken over by climbers who probably are at their most numerous in the autumn. It is said that on a fine Sunday there are queues to scale the more popular climbs even though there are over 500 recognised climbing routes.

The walk starts at the county boundary near Moscar Lodge on the A57 (SK 231 879) not far from the Strines road.

From the public footpath signpost walk due south on the prominent path gradually ascending towards the start of Stanage Edge. Follow the path to the track rising from Bamford. Mill-stones will be seen before reaching the track. The path keeps to the underside of the edge, at times veering away from the edge. The track joined was a Roman road that connected Doncaster and Buxton; that particular section being between Templeborough and Brough, near Hope.

Turn left and climb the track that gradually veers away from Stanage Edge rising to Stanage Pole at the top of the hill. Continue down the other side of the hill to join Redmires Reservoir road. Walk along the road and after the right bend, just past Redmires car park and picnic area turn left through a stile at a public footpath signpost, into a wood and climb the hill through the trees with a wall to your right. The trees are soon left behind and the path continues over fields, then moorland.

When the wall turns sharp right carry on forward to the next wall, keeping it to your left. Descend and cross the reservoir drain and the stile beyond to continue on the path down to the wooded valley below. Cross by the bridge and climb the hill to emerge on to the A57 at a public footpath signpost.

Cross the road and take the track to the right of a farm at another public footpath signpost. On entering the field beyond the track ascend the field to the wall stile visible from the last gate. Climb the next field to join a metalled road until it turns sharp left. Leave the road to continue in the same direction as before on a beaten earth track that gradually veers left, passing to the right of a farm. At a T junction at the parish boundary stone turn left and return to the A57 passing Moscar Lodge to return to the starting place.

CHATSWORTH PARK

WALK 10

★

4 miles (6.5 km)

OS Landranger 119, White Peak

Chatsworth House is one of the stateliest of buildings and its gardens are equally elegant. It is the seat of the Duke of Devonshire. The main part was built between 1686 and 1707 by the first duke and succeeding descendants have modified and added to the house. At the other side of the river is a public footpath and the walk by the river gives excellent views of the house as does the descent from the top of the walk.

Edensor adjoins the park and is one of Derbyshire's model villages. Each house is of a different design as ordered by one of the dukes. The walk starts at the Calton Lees car park, close to the Chatsworth Garden Centre (SK 258 687).

Continue on the road that passes through the car park and continues past the garden centre and beyond that to the Chatsworth Forestry works. When the road reverts to a gravelled track at a cross roads pass through the gate ahead to walk up the valley track to Calton Houses. Here the track zigzags round the buildings eventually reaching the top of the hill to cross on level ground to a wood. The track enters the wood, descends and a gate lower down permits you to enter open ground with marvellous views across Chatsworth Park and Chatsworth House.

Aim to the left of a major copse halfway down the hill and for Edensor church beyond at the bottom of the hill. Just to the left of the churchyard is the entry to Edensor village down steps to the village street. Turn right and walk to the main

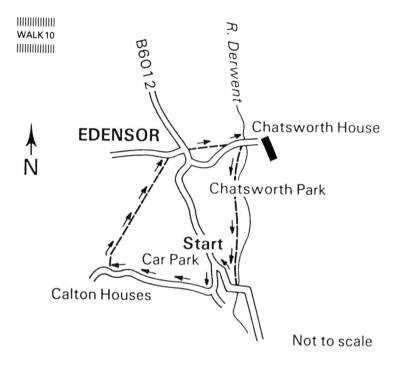

Not to scale

road through the park passing the church on the way and reaching the road after passing through large gates.

Cross the road and take the made path at the other side to walk over the brow of the hill and down to the bridge carrying the road to Chatsworth House. Turn right at the bridge to take the river path back to the car park. The path is about 1½ miles long.

HIGH PEAK AND
TISSINGTON TRAILS

WALK 11

★

6½ miles (10.5 km)

OS Landranger 119, White Peak

The High Peak and Tissington Trails are the remains of railway systems converted by the Peak Park Planning Board for use by walkers, horse riders and cyclists. The tracks have been gravelled or grassed and the stations converted into car parks and picnic areas. The High Peak Trail was the longest of the two systems and was built to provide a link between the Cromford Canal in the south and Peak Forest Canal at Whaley Bridge. It was never a profitable concern.

The walk starts at the Parsley Hay station, just off the A515 road (SK 147 637). It is now a picnic area, car park and cycle hire centre.

Walk south on the old railway track and when the track splits take the left fork along the High Peak Trail. The cutting on the right fork is on the Tissington Trail and will be visited on the return journey. At this junction, on the ground, is a direction indicator. Continue on the High Peak Trail as far as Friden.

On the Ashbourne road bridge arch is a stone engraving about the High Peak railway. Friden is recognised long before it is reached, for the chimneys of the DSF Refractories brick works at Friden stand out in the distance. Just past the brick works is Friden station, now a picnic area and car park.

Turn right at Friden station on to the road passing under the railway bridge and walk to the A5012 and beyond to the

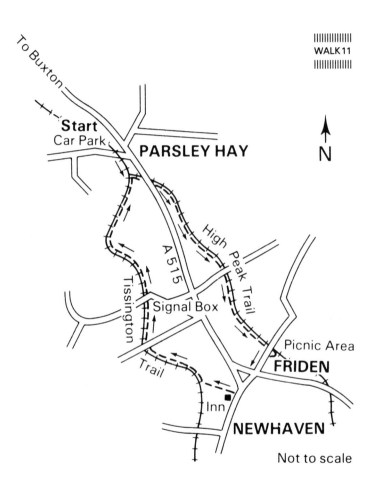

To Buxton

Start
Car Park

PARSLEY HAY

N

High Peak Trail

A 515

Tissington

Signal Box

Trail

Picnic Area

FRIDEN

Inn

NEWHAVEN

Not to scale

38

Ashbourne–Buxton A515 road. Turn left on the A515 and just before the Newhaven Hotel turn right over a stile at the signpost 'Public Footpath to Heathcote 2'.

The walk is now across fields as far as the Tissington Trail. Having passed into the field beyond the buildings close to the hotel, bear left to the stile in the wall beyond the low power lines. Go over the stile and bear right to a stile in the wall opposite bringing you to the right of more buildings. Cross the fields ahead to join a farm track crossing a field. The track emerges from the farm.

Follow the track until it passes between two walls, behind which are trees, then following the direction of the footpath signpost 'Footpath to Heathcote, to Trail', descend obliquely to eventually pass over a stile on to the Tissington Trail.

The trail can be seen from the signpost, as can a bridge directly down the hill, but ignore the bridge as it is not the way on to the trail. Turn right and follow the Tissington Trail back to Parsley Hay, passing Hartington station on the way. Here is another picnic area, car park and signal box used as an information bureau.

WIN HILL

WALK 12

★

5 miles (8 km)

OS Landranger 110, Dark Peak

Legend has it that in AD 626 Edwin, King of Northumberland camped on Win Hill and Cynegil and Cuichem, Kings of Wessex, camped on Lose Hill. The ensuing battle between the two kingdoms, besides deciding the fate of many men, also gave the peaks their names.

Win Hill at 1,517 ft is not as high as some in the Peak Park, but views from its summit can hardly be equalled. They are spectacular. The walk starts from Hope car park (SK 171 835).

Take the Edale road opposite Hope church and walk as far as the Hope county primary school sports field and turn right, down the road to Killhill bridge. The turning is near a house called Kilncroft.

Walk along the road and after passing under the railway bridge turn left. At the drive to 'The Homestead' take the stile to the left of the gate and on to the dirt road ahead. After 100 yards pass through another stile into a field and continue in the same direction with a wall on the right. There are now open views and to the immediate left is Lose Hill and Mam Tor further over.

Pass through Fullwood Stile Farm and take the road beyond, now climbing up a steady incline. Beyond the gate at the end of the road, which becomes a track, turn right up a steeper path gradually leaving the other path. Almost 50 yards before a large plantation turn right on to another track

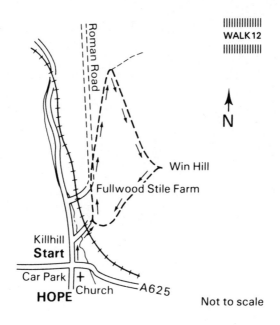

WALK 12

N

Win Hill

Fullwood Stile Farm

Roman Road

Killhill
Start

Car Park
HOPE Church A625

Not to scale

and walk on it to the top of Win Hill. This is a well-used path with cairns along the way.

After visiting the peak retrace your steps and turn left down a broad, cairn-marked path. When farm land is reached continue descending directly downhill and at a ruined building pass through a gate to join a track beyond and continue descending until the track reaches a road at a railway bridge. Turn left under the bridge and at the Edale road turn left to return to Hope.

41

LOSE HILL

WALK 13

★

6½ miles (10.5 km)

OS Landranger 110, Dark Peak

Lose Hill at 1,563 ft is slightly higher than Win Hill, its partner down the valley. The summit is National Trust property. The walk starts at the Castleton car park (SK 149 830).

Leave the car park by the eastern exit, usable only by pedestrians, and turn left along the road. At the Hollowford Training Centre, about ½ mile along the road take the left fork signposted 'Hollins Cross'. The path to the skyline is now more distinct. At the foot of the hills leave the road and take the path to the right and climb up to Hollins Cross at the top of the path.

Turn right and walk on the path along the ridge, climbing Black Tor and later Lose Hill. Descend the mountain towards Hope, visible to the south east, and after climbing a stile at a National Trust sign and just beyond a large, flat cairn, take the path to the left of a broken wall and descend to the valley bottom. The path enters a farm road and finally finishes up on the Edale valley road. Turn right and walk into Hope, reaching the small town at a church.

Before leaving Hope have a look at the church, in particular the outside. If gargoyles are working correctly no evil spirits dare enter a church. Hope church, on that proviso, must be the holiest building in the kingdom, according to the gargoyles on the south face. Perhaps you might agree after seeing them.

Take the road to the west of the church and at the road fork, bear right and almost at once turn right over a stile into

42

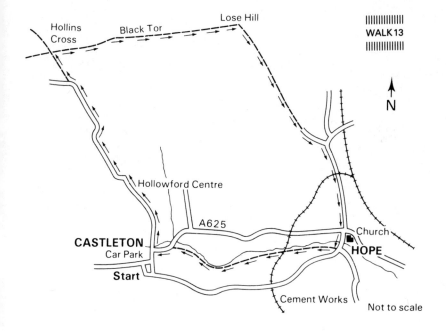

a field. Now take a path that follows Peakhole Water to join the main valley road just to the east of Castleton. The path basically follows the river, crossing the railway track leading to the nearby APCM cement works, and eventually joins the road leading back into Castleton.

43

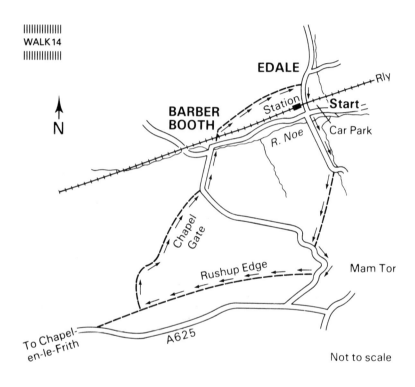

||||||||||||||
WALK 14
||||||||||||||

↑
N

EDALE

BARBER BOOTH

Station

Start

Car Park

R. Noe

Rly

Chapel Gate

Rushup Edge

Mam Tor

To Chapel-en-le-Frith

A625

Not to scale

RUSHUP EDGE

WALK 14

★

6 miles (9.5 km)

OS Landranger 110, Dark Peak

To the south of Edale is an inviting ridge. Far to the east is Lose Hill. Next to this peak is Black Tor. Directly above is Mam Tor, and then stretching on to the west is Rushup Edge. If you have good eyesight you will more than likely see tiny figures silhouetted against the sky. They are walking where you hope to walk. From the edge, which is a high ridge, running parallel with the Castleton–Chapel-en-le-Frith A625 road are splendid views, particularly of the Vale of Edale and to the north Kinder Scout.

The walk starts at Edale car park (SK 124 853) close to Edale railway station. Looking towards Mam Tor, just to the west, is a dip in the skyline. This is the immediate objective.

Leaving the car park main entrance, turn right to walk along the valley road and turn left on to a narrow farm road at a signpost 'Public Bridleway, Castleton'. Cross the river Noe and walk on the farm road until just before the road goes left over a stream. Take the path to the right of the road and after a few yards go over a ladder stile into the field beyond. Take the path which makes a beeline for the hill above, eventually reaching the road that descends from the A625 to Edale. Turn left up the road and when it swings left take the stile to the right to continue climbing. This merely cuts out the zigzag of the road. When the path meets the road again, follow the signpost's instruction and climb on to Rushup Edge.

When on the edge there is still a gradual climb. After the

45

top of the ridge has been reached and the land begins to fall away, there are no longer unrestricted views to the north.

Just after the A625 becomes visible look out for a signpost indicating where the path leads. Turn right on a joining path to start the inward walk and descend Chapel Gate to the Edale road. At first, walking is on level ground, but gradually the path begins its long, downward route. Ignore other paths that veer off in unlikely directions. Turn left at the road and descend to Barber Booth, a hamlet with a few houses. When the road turns right leave it to take the narrower road leading to houses and a shop.

This small road soon swings back to rejoin the Edale road, but just before the roads meet, turn left up a track at the signpost 'Public Footpath, Grindsbrook 1'. After crossing the railway turn right through a stile and cross the fields to Edale.

The path is roughly parallel with the railway and is way-marked on stiles and well-used, emerging into the road leading to Grindsbrook Booth from the car park, at Champion House, not far from the Edale tourist information centre, which is also the mountain rescue headquarters. Turn right and return to the car park.

CHINLEY CHURN

WALK 15

★

6 miles (9.5 km)

OS Landranger 110, Dark Peak

Chinley Churn at 1,480 feet is a not very well known minor mountain, undiscovered and away from the crowds. It provides the setting for a walk that affords marvellous views around the surrounding area, in particular Hayfield, New Mills and Whaley Bridge.

The walk starts at the highest point of the A624 Hayfield – Chapel-en-le-Frith road (SK 049 850). There is a parking lay-by just to the south.

Take the track at the sign 'Footpath to Birch Vale' and just beyond the gate of the farm ahead turn right into a field at the signpost 'To Birch Vale and Hayfield via Phoside and Ridge Top'. Head for the pylon across the field and after this walk to the left of a wall underneath the hillside. Do not take an inviting path that gradually rises up the hill, but keep to the wall side passing over a stile into a field. Cross the field, keeping parallel with the wall above, gradually falling to a farm almost hidden in trees. When this is reached keep to the left of the farm boundary wall and continue as far as a wood.

Just before the stile into the wood turn left on to another path to skirt the wood to eventually join and cross a stream. Over the stream join a path climbing the hill keeping to the left of a wall. When the top of the hill is reached a radio mast can be seen; this will shortly be passed. When a farm road is joined, turn left on the track heading for the mast and at the wall beyond make for a wooden pylon ahead. This is the start

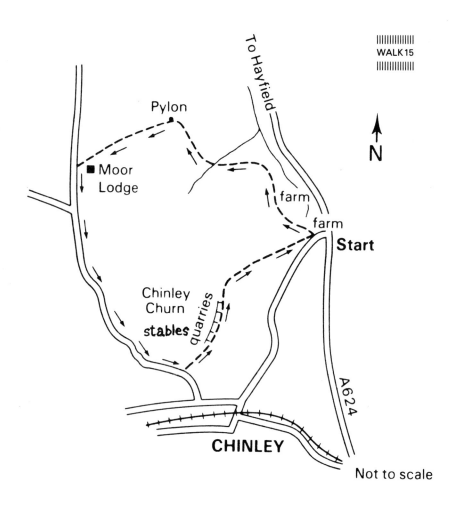

WALK 15

N

To Hayfield

Pylon

Moor Lodge

farm

farm

Start

Chinley Churn

stables quarries

A624

CHINLEY

Not to scale

48

of a series of pylons carrying low power lines. At the first pole make for trees in the distance. These enclose a group of buildings, including Moor Lodge. At the unmade lane turn left and walk for about 2 miles. When the lane forks take the left turn.

The next turning point is on the steep descending road well beyond some stables to the left of the track. When within sight of a farm below climb over a stile at a public footpath signpost and climb the path to the quarries which lie beneath the Ordnance Survey column on top of Chinley Churn. The path soon passes under the old workings, then through them, eventually climbing up, but never actually reaching the highest ground. Here there are bits of old machinery once used in the extensive, but now abandoned, workings.

After passing the quarry the path continues along the hillside and at a building joins a track that gradually descends the hill to the starting place.

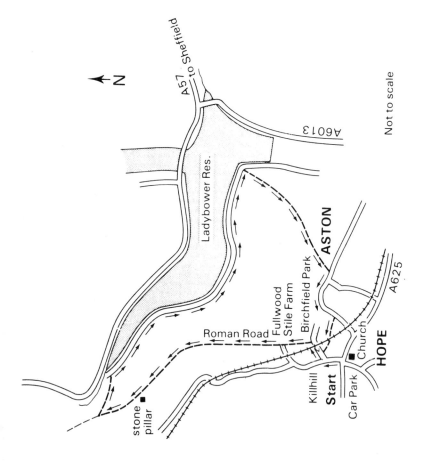

AROUND WIN HILL

WALK 16

★

9 miles (14.5 km)

OS Landranger 110, Dark Peak

Ladybower Reservoir was the last of a series of reservoirs to be constructed in the Derwent area. Started in 1935 and completed in 1943 the reservoir holds 6,300 million gallons of water and is one of the largest in Britain. Overlooking the reservoir is Win Hill and around this peak is the walk, a long stretch being on the hard track that constitutes one of the reservoir roads. The walk starts at Hope car park (SK 171 835).

Starting as for Walk 12, take the Edale road opposite Hope church and walk as far as the Hope county primary school sports field and turn right down the road to Killhill bridge. The turning is near a house called Kilncroft. Walk along the road and after passing under the railway bridge turn left. At the drive to 'The Homestead' take the stile to the left of the gate and go on to the dirt road ahead. After 100 yards, pass through another stile into a field and continue in the same direction with a wall on the right. There are now open views and to the immediate left is Lose Hill with Mam Tor further over.
   Pass through Fullwood Stile Farm and take the road beyond, now climbing up a steady incline. Beyond the gate at the end of the road take the dirt track ahead and continue the easy ascent. This is the Roman road from the Roman fort at Brough to that at Melandra near Glossop. Soon to the left is a good view of the Vale of Edale.

After 1½ miles a stone pillar is passed. Names of towns are engraved on the top stone. Shortly after, the old road joins another path at a signpost. Turn right to take the Haggside path and descend through the plantation towards the valley below. At a bridleway sign some way down the hill, follow the arrow on the sign, but look for a stile further down at a sharp, left turn and climb it to enter the plantation. Follow the path to join the beaten earth road below. Turn right and follow the road.

Very soon the road reaches Ladybower Reservoir, and altogether 2 miles are walked on the reservoir road. The next turning is at the ruins of a farm within sight of Ashopton Viaduct. The ruins are found after climbing from the reservoir side and just before the road enters a plantation down the other side of the rise.

Turn right at the farm ruins on a grass track and after a few yards, left to make a gradual ascent through the plantation of mature pines and evergreens. At the first forest crossroads continue forward. At the second forest crossroads bear right, all the time gradually rising. These crossroads are merely tracks used by forest workers. The track gradually narrows to become a path and at the end of the plantation, at a stile, continues up the hillside. Here the world opens out high above the Bamford road. Ladybower Reservoir can be seen well below to the left and Bamford Edge seen across the other side of the valley.

Ascend the hillside on the path until it joins a broader path. The path now begins to descend, but at a farm gate turns right, up the hill again until another path is joined. Turn left and climb the stile to follow the ditch beyond. Further down the hill a stile is climbed and the descent is continued into Aston. Turn right to walk on the road through the hamlet. At the Fairfield Farm road next to a detached bungalow called Meadowbank turn right and gradually descend, skirting Birchfield Park until the road at Killhill Bridge is reached. Turn left and return to Hope.

ERRWOOD RESERVOIR

WALK 17

★

4 miles (6.5 km)

OS Landranger 119, White Peak

Errwood Reservoir is the newest of the two Goyt Valley reservoirs, being completed in 1967. The walk starts at the car park at the foot of the reservoir on the western side (SK 013 757). Anyone descending to the Goyt Valley from the Macclesfield road should start the walk at Goytsclough

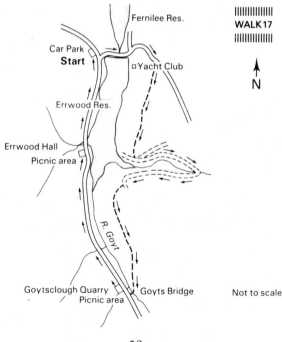

Quarry (SK 012 734) as there is a one way system in operation along the side of the reservoir.

Take the road across the foot of the reservoir and continue up the hill past the toilets. After passing a plantation turn right at the signpost 'No.4 Goyts Clough' to follow the path across a field to another plantation. When the plantation is passed carry on walking to reach a track following a narrow valley eventually crossing the stream and heading back towards the reservoir.

At an ascending left bend turn right at a footpath sign to join a path which eventually approaches the water and then follows the river Goyt until the bridge at Goytsclough Quarry is reached. In places the way is quite boggy especially during a wet spell.

Cross to the road, turn right and walk all the way back to the car park, now on the western side of the river Goyt and Errwood Reservoir.

RIVER GOYT

WALK 18

★

6 miles (9.5 km)

OS Landranger 119, White Peak

The river Goyt flows from south to north rising not far from the Cat and Fiddle inn and flows into Errwood Reservoir, the newest of the Goyt Valley reservoirs. By its side is the road also starting near the Cat and Fiddle, but, under present traffic arrangements, this is a one way road from the reservoir to Derbyshire Bridge. Errwood Reservoir holds 935 million gallons of water and is a yachting reservoir.

The walk starts at the Goyts Lane car park on the eastern heights above the Goyt Valley (SK 024 752). This is reached down a narrow road from the Buxton – Whaley Bridge B5002 road and is next to a pond.

Walk past the pond and turn left on to the old railway track. Once part of the Cromford and High Peak railway system this section has been converted into a delightful, wide grass path that contours the hill. When the track reaches a bricked-up tunnel, strike left up the hill on a path with a wall to your left and when near to the top bear slightly right with the path and attendant marker posts to a ladder stile over a wall.

In the distance can be seen limestone peaks from quarry workings. In front of these is the village of Burbage, merging into Buxton to the east. Ahead and to the right can be seen the continuations of the railway track after its emergence from the tunnel. Below to the left of the track is the road leading to Burbage.

Descend by the path to the road below, turn right and walk

55

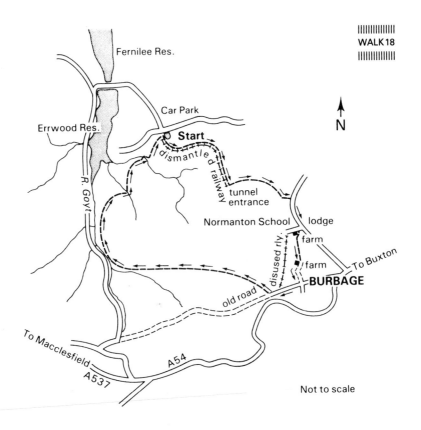

Not to scale

as far as a solitary house on the left. This would apparently be a lodge. Opposite the house is a narrow road, the drive to Normanton school. Next to it is another narrow road. Take this and turn left on to a drive prior to a farm. Take a stile on the left into a field and walk away from the farm to the stile in a wall. Beyond this, walk on the right hand side of another wall and enter a large copse. At the far side of the wood is another stile and the path is now over fields and stiles to a farm. Pass through the farm on to the farm road. When the farm road reaches a road at a crossroads turn right and

56

walk up the hill. This soon reverts to a wide, stony track and is in fact the old Macclesfield road.

After passing the disused railway track, turn right through a stile at the signpost 'Public Footpath to Lamaload via Shining Tor' and take the path following a wall with a wood at the other side. When the wall turns right take the path that ascends the hill in the same direction, but gradually leaving it and heading for more trees on the horizon. The path can be seen climbing to a stile to the left of the trees.

Through the stile the path now is over open moorland at first on level ground and then leisurely descending to the river Goyt. Before leaving the top of the hill look to the skyline to the west. The solitary building is the Cat and Fiddle inn, the second highest inn in England.

Two bridges are passed on the walk down the valley. The second is Goyts bridge and nearby is a picnic site. Stay on the eastern side of the river and on the path that rises a little from the water. When Errwood reservoir comes into view the path bears right to join a stony track at a footpath sign. Turn left down the hill. The track gradually levels to follow another valley. Up on the skyline to the left can be seen the straight line of the railway embankment.

After crossing the stream turn right on the path signposted 'Goyts Lane Car Park' and shortly afterwards climb the hill as indicated by a similar signpost to return to the car park.

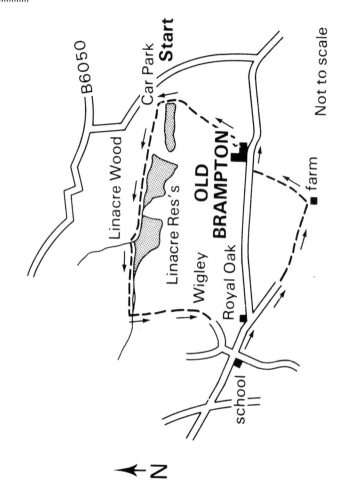

LINACRE WOOD

WALK 19

★

5 miles (8 km)

OS Landranger 119, White Peak

Linacre Wood is a Chesterfield beauty spot with three reservoirs and in spring a carpet of bluebells. There are concessionary paths round all the reservoirs and all these are to be seen on a map in one of the car parks on the approach to the reservoirs. Towards the end of the walk the attractive village of Old Brampton is visited, taking in the church of St Peter and St Paul with its battlemented walls, octagonal spire, two lych gates and Norman origins.

The walk starts at a car park reached by the water authority's narrow road from the B6050, about ½ mile west of Cutthorpe. The car park is one to the right of the lane almost before the reservoir is reached (SK 338 726).

Descend through the wood and turn right along a track just below the car park and continue on it as far as the third reservoir. Take the path alongside the reservoir and at its head continue on the path following the stream until a log stile at the end of the wood is reached. Continue across the field ahead joining a descending path which turns west. Along the fields a descending stream is crossed by concrete stepping stones and later the east-flowing stream itself is crossed by a small, old bridge.

At the other side of the bridge is a stream coming from a wooded valley. Take the path on the eastern side of the stream that gradually climbs almost parallel with the stream, but ascends much higher. When the path emerges from the wood at a stile and a gateway ignore both to take a fainter path to the right that descends slightly at first then gradually ascends as an old walled and fenced grass track overgrown in places, the overgrown parts being easily avoided. In the distance can be seen a farm. When reached pass it to its right by a stile to join a farm road at Wigley Farm. Walk on the road to join the main road at a school.

Turn left on the Old Brampton road then right on the narrow road opposite The Royal Oak. When the second farm is reached the road turns sharp right to avoid the farm and it has now reverted to grass. About 50 yards before the third farm, enter a field to the left and make for a wall stile diagonally across the field almost at the bottom at the far wall. Follow the path beyond through a wood and cross the stream by an old, stone bridge. Climb up through the wood and walk along the left side of a field. Repeat this over the next four fields ignoring a path leaving the wall in the second field. Join the road and turn right into Old Brampton.

At the church of St Peter and St Paul walk through the church-yard to the northeast corner of the grounds and take the stiles on to a path heading towards the wood. A field length away from the wood cross the field diagonally to enter the wood at a signpost 'To Cutthorpe'. Shortly through the wood cross the foot of the first Linacre reservoir and climb up the steps beyond to the road. Turn left and return to the car park.

CROWDECOTE

WALK 20

9 miles (14.5 km)

OS Landranger 119, White Peak

The river Dove rises near the A53 Leek–Buxton road not far from the village of Flash and, incidentally about ½ mile from the source of the river Manifold. For much of the way the Dove forms a natural boundary between Staffordshire and Derbyshire. Below Hartington the valley gains several identities. First Beresford Dale, then Wolfscote Dale, then Dove Dale itself. At Crowdecote the river is narrow with the proportions of a stream and remains so for some distance.

Crowdecote lies off the river Dove about 1 mile east of Longnor. Its claim to fame is a mention in the Domesday Book, an achievement not given to all. The walk itself is across agricultural land, alongside the river and a walk along the High Peak Trail. There is a stretch of road walking of 1¾ miles, but the road is seldom used, indeed grass grows on it in places.

The walk starts at Parsley Hay picnic area (SK 147 637), a busy place on a sunny Sunday, as this is a cycle hire centre. This is close to the Buxton – Ashbourne A515 trunk road slightly nearer Buxton than Ashbourne.

Walk to the car park entrance and turn right down the road passing under the railway bridge. On reaching Darley Farm find a waymarked stile and walk with a wall to your right crossing fields and waymarked stiles and through gates until Vincent House Farm is reached at another road. Cross the road and beyond a wall stile climb the hill continuing in the

61

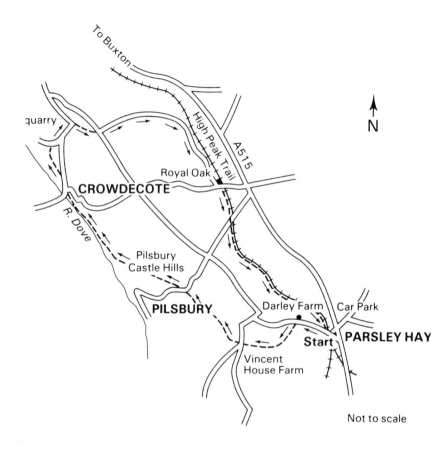

same direction as the approach to Vincent House. On clearing the brow of the short hill head for the field corner and its stile. This is just to the right of power lines.

Cross the next field parallel with the power lines and, at a pond encroaching on to four fields, bear slightly left to cross more fields down the middle of a shallow valley passing a solitary, upright rock before joining a narrow road a few yards to the right of a farm track. Turn right and at the barn a few yards on turn left into the field continuing in the same direction as before.

This is now across a pathless field and if there is doubt about the way bear left to join a road or a track to the southwest.

Contour the hill and when the valley begins to open out in front, start to descend and beyond a wall join a track near the rocky hill known as Pilsbury Castle Hills. Follow the track and just before it reaches the river turn right, cross over a stile and walk parallel with the course of the river until Crowdecote is reached.

Turn right, passing the Pack Horse inn. Take the first left road turn and after a short walk left again to walk along a farm track, then past the farm ahead to walk again parallel with the river. When a track is joined turn right towards a gorge seen earlier and at the road turn left to walk up the middle of a narrow ravine. When the road begins to bend left at an old quarry turn right through a gateway to climb an old track. At a stagnant pool turn left to join a road. The old quarry below is quite popular with rock climbers.

Turn right along the road then almost at once turn left up a narrower road. Continue on it until it crosses the High Peak Trail at the Royal Oak inn. Join the trail and walk back to Parsley Hay.

HARTINGTON

WALK 21

★

5 miles (8 km)

OS Landranger 119, White Peak

Hartington is an attractive village popular with walkers and casual visitors alike, lying as it does near the river Dove. The walk is over mainly agricultural land with the higher views on the return leg. The walk starts in the village itself (SK 129 604).

Walk to the lane below the church, turn left and walk along the road until a concrete and corrugated building on the left its reached. Turn left through a stile and pass round the building into a field beyond.

The way ahead is now over farm land and, as ever, navigation means finding stiles. Generally the going is level, but if navigation does go astray descend to the narrow road below and walk along to Pilsbury. Field by field description is as follows.

Cross to the opposite wall. Pass over a wall stile. Cross a field to a stile to the right of two trees. Go over a stile and on to the next stile in a wall corner. Turn left with the wall to a gate. Pass through a gate at a track and follow the wall on the grass to the next wall-corner stile. Continue alongside the wall until the wall turns sharp right. Below can be seen the Pilsbury road. Ahead is an open hillside with short trees here and there.

Go forward in the same direction and, on reaching a track, follow it until it disappears. Carry on in the same direction, keeping at the same level but erring to the higher ground and

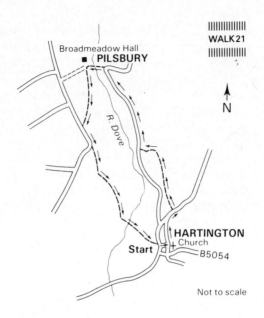

Broadmeadow Hall
■ (PILSBURY

R. Dove

N

HARTINGTON
Church
Start
B5054

Not to scale

eventually taking a wooden stile in an opposing wall 50 yards below the wall at the foot of steeper slopes. Beyond are old mine workings. Turn down the hill to pass through the gateway in a wall corner. Descend the next field to join the Pilsbury road below. Turn right on the road and walk to Pilsbury.

After passing a farm turn left down a track and cross the river. Follow the track until the gate leading to Broadmeadow Hall is reached. Turn left into the field opposite and head diagonally up the field towards several trees on the skyline. One hundred yards below the trees turn left through a stile and walk along the hillside to take another stile three quarters of the way on the wall to your right. Head now for the stile to be seen in the next field, but one near more trees. Beyond the stile which leads into a narrow field with a barn, pass the barn and locate the next stile halfway along a hedge and join a road.

Walk along the road to the farm ahead then join the footpath as indicated to the right of the buildings and walk across four fields with a wall to your right. After the last field when there is no more wall to follow strike directly for Hartington now seen ahead and when able to see the fields below descend to the next stile. The path beyond is again to the left of a wall and after a short way runs along the top of a plantation.

Beyond the wood descend the hill diagonally towards a farm. When a fence is reached below, turn left over a stile and cross the field to the river. Once over the river follow the path across fields to a clean-looking factory, and back to Hartington.

DOVE HOLES

WALK 22

★

6 miles (9.5 km)

OS Landranger 119, White Peak

The section of Dove Dale covered in this walk is between Dove Holes in the south and Iron Tors in the north. Dove Holes is the largest cave in Dove Dale and is close to the riverside path. The Tissington Trail provides the connecting link for the paths to and from the river.

The walk starts at the Alsop Moor Cottages car park (SK 157 564). This is really a small lay-by on the A515 Ashbourne – Buxton road.

Take the Tissington Trail at the other side of the A515 and walk south as far as the Alsop-en-le-Dale car park and picnic area. Cross the A515 at that point and go through the stile at the signpost 'Public Footpath, Dove Dale via Nabs Dale 1¼'. Cross the field in the direction of a farm road visible across the field. When reached take the track, which is at the other side of a narrow road signed 'New Hanson Grange'. When the track begins to descend, strike left across the field at a footpath sign to another signpost at a stile. The turning off place is just before a farm.

After passing through the stile descend to the gate ahead and below and take the stile next to it. This is in effect a by-pass of the farm. Follow the wall on the right and by the path descend to the river Dove. On reaching the river turn left for a few yards to see Dove Holes, then walk upstream on the riverside path as far as Milldale, a small village on the western bank. Cross the river to the village and walk along the road

67

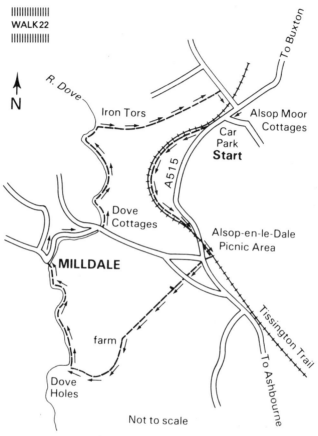

N

R. Dove

To Buxton

Iron Tors

Alsop Moor
Cottages

Car
Park
Start

A515

Dove
Cottages

Alsop-en-le-Dale
Picnic Area

MILLDALE

Tissington Trail

farm

To Ashbourne

Dove
Holes

Not to scale

still upstream to the next bridge at Dove Cottages. Join the
river path on the eastern bank at the sign 'Public Footpath,
Wolfscote Dale 2'.

At an official-looking, small building with a double pad-
locked door just before a wooden footbridge turn right up a
dry valley keeping the wall to your right. Later, beyond the
trees transfer to the other side of the wall and eventually join
a minor road, near the railway embankment. Turn right and
at the A515 return to the car park.

DOVE DALE

WALK 23

★

5½ miles (9 km)

OS Landranger 119, White Peak

Dove Dale is one of the undoubted beauty spots of North Derbyshire. It is a narrow, wooded valley with limestone towers and fissures creating a magnificent dale. Because of their shapes several features are named on maps. Dovedale Castles, Twelve Apostles, Lovers Leap, Tissington Spires, Reynard's Cave and Ilam Rock are a few to be seen on the way. Reynard's Cave, in particular, lying above the path to the right is at first a high arch and higher up a cave.

The walk starts at the Dove Dale car park at the bottom of the dale (SK 145 507). Dove Dale is signposted from the A515 Ashbourne – Buxton road.

Walk up the path parallel to the road and cross the river by the first bridge to continue on the path at the other side. Walk upstream for about 2 miles to the next bridge. At times the path leaves the stream, but always returns. At Ilam Rock, a massive, single pillar of limestone rising from the western bank, cross the river by the log and wooden bridge and continue upstream on another path. When an open, dry valley appears take the path up the middle of the valley and gradually climb to the fields above.

After climbing a stile and when the houses of Stanshope can be seen locate a stile on the left, just before another stile directly ahead and climb the hill with a wall to your right. On the level walk forward by the wall and, just beyond a group of trees, turn right up a walled grass track to the road visible

69

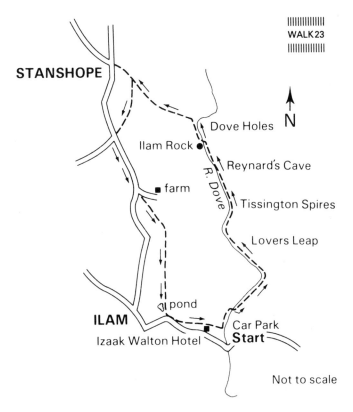

STANSHOPE

Dove Holes

N

Ilam Rock ●

Reynard's Cave

R. Dove

■ farm

Tissington Spires

Lovers Leap

pond

ILAM

Car Park
Start

Izaak Walton Hotel

Not to scale

near the houses. This is a minor road from Alstonefield to Ilam. On reaching the road turn left and walk south. After walking for about ½ mile look out for an open farm road on the left. This is about 200 yards before a group of trees and two road signs. Pass over a cattle grid in the farm road and just beyond the next gateway bear half right and walk towards the extreme left of a group of trees. When these are reached climb over a stile in the wall ahead and descend to the next stile beyond and to the left of the trees.

After climbing into the next field head for the valley bottom and the pond just visible through the trees, always keeping to

70

the left of the wall. Over to the right is the picturesque village of Ilam. When a track is reached near the road below turn left at the sign 'Public Footpath to Dovedale'. When the track stops at the gate ahead carry on across the next field, making for the left of the second group of buildings. This is the Izaak Walton Hotel. Once past the hotel out-buildings, the Dove Dale car park can be seen and easily reached.

THORPE
MAPLETON

WALK 24

★

5 miles (8 km)

OS Landranger 119

Just below Thorpe the river Dove passes out of the Peak Park and with the addition of the water from the river Manifold becomes a wider river. The walk is along the section between Mapleton and Thorpe.

Thorpe and Mapleton are two charming villages just off the river Dove. Thorpe is probably the oldest, being once a Danish settlement. Its church has a Norman tower and nave and close by are several old buildings. Mapleton has a curious old church with old glass and a narrow staircase leading to a miniature gallery.

The outward journey is on the Tissington Trail mainly on an elevated embankment and starts at the Thorpe picnic site and car park on the Tissington Trail (SK 166 505). This is reached from the A515 Buxton–Ashbourne road by taking the road signposted Thorpe and at the sharp right turn prior to the Dog and Partridge leaving the road to follow the 'P' sign to the Thorpe picnic site, where the car may be left.

Walk south along the Tissington Trail and just before the track goes over a river turn right down some steps at a small Tissington Trail sign.

The next stage is a beeline over fields and stiles until the road into Mapleton is reached; directions as follows.

Climb the field beyond the steps and go over the stile near the top right hand corner. Continue up the next field close to

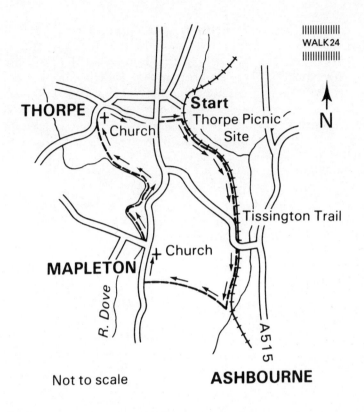

THORPE

Start

Thorpe Picnic
Site

+ Church

Tissington Trail

N

+ Church

MAPLETON

R. Dove

A515

Not to scale

ASHBOURNE

a hedge on your left. Climb over the stile which is adjacent to a gate about 20 yards to the right of the field corner, and on to a stile over the next field, now with a hedge to your right. Forward across another field with a hedge to the right. Bear slightly right across the next field to the stile in the opposing hedge and down the field beyond, with a hedge to your right. The river Dove can now be seen beyond the houses and road below. Descend the field, over a stile across another field and on to the road to the right of the houses.

The directions appear complicated but unfortunately directing walkers over agricultural land is complicated, as

73

there are always many fields to cross. The rule in this walk is keep in the same direction looking ahead to the next stile.

Turn right and walk along the road towards Mapleton. Opposite the Okeover Arms, next to the church, turn left into a field at the signpost 'Public Footpath to Dovedale' and walk towards the river bridge. Just before the bridge enter and cross the road to climb the stile into a field. Follow the river footpath until a wood is reached then climb through the trees and up the field ahead to the village of Thorpe, entering there to the left of houses. Just before leaving the river, the village is visible from the river path.

Turn right into Thorpe and just past the church turn right down the hill. After passing the post office at the bottom, turn right on the narrow road, at first descending then climbing the hill ahead. On reaching the next road climb the stile at the other side of the road and cross fields and stiles to rejoin the Tissington Trail. Turn left and return to the car park.

MILLER'S DALE
MONSAL DALE

WALK 25

★

7 miles (11 km)

OS Landranger 119, White Peak

The river Wye rises not far from the Cheshire border, passes through Buxton, wanders across Derbyshire, passes through Bakewell and joins the south bound Derwent at Rowsley. The Wye passes through beautiful countryside and the walk is by it for part of the way, in the valley between the foot of Tideswell Dale and the A6. Besides the beauty to behold there is the history to absorb, particularly in the valley.

The picturesque hamlet of Upperdale to the north west of Little Longstone is the starting point (SK 178 721).

Walk on the road towards Little Longstone as far as the sign that warns of a steep hill (one in six). High on the hill ahead can be seen Monsal Head Hotel at a renowned viewpoint. Cross the river by the bridge visible from the road, turn left and walk on the path until the stile immediately before the Buxton – Bakewell A6 road.

On the path a viaduct of a disused railway is soon passed. Further downstream there is an attractive weir where it may be possible to see a dipper, a small river bird easily recognisable by its white throat.

Just before the A6 is reached turn right up a narrow path signposted 'Public Footpath to Brushfield' zigzagging up the hill through the trees eventually emerging on to open fields high above the valley. This is part of one of the Peak Park's

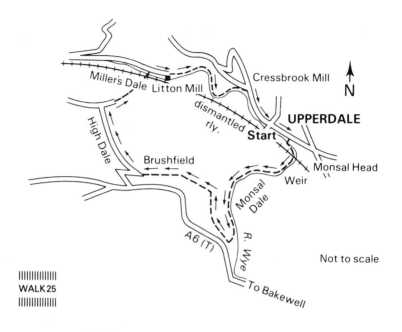

recommended long walks and frequent yellow markers can be seen along the way from Monsal Dale to Miller's Dale.

At the top of the hill climb over the wall stile and walk towards the farm ahead. Just before the farm bear left through a gate as indicated by signs. Pass through the farm yard and turn right up the farm road beyond farm buildings. Continue on the track over the fields and at the junction turn left. This is signposted to Brushfield. Walk on the track until several farm buildings are passed and a road is joined. This section of the road is high above the A6 at Taddington Dale.

Turn right and walk on the farm road. This is a gated track and follows High Dale to the left for ¾ mile. The track is for the next part over open ground, but the last section beyond a gate is through trees and the track becomes overgrown. At a sharp left bend take a stile to the right into Priestcliffe Lees Nature Reserve and walk across the narrow field. Open views across the valley are soon reached. The field sharply descends and below in the right of the field a stile is taken. Descend diagonally down the hill to enter Miller's Dale near Litton Mill. Turn right and walk along the road to Litton Mill. The original mill was built in 1782 by Ellis Needham of Haregate Hall near Tideswell and his partner Thomas Frith, a Tideswell farmer. The mill was virtually run on the slave labour of orphaned children and became thoroughly notorious for the inhumane treatment meted out by the masters to the children, some as young as nine years old.

Pass down the mill yard and on to the river path and walk to the next mill and road beyond. This section of the Wye is Water-cum-Jolly Dale. At the bottom is the imposing Georgian structure of Cressbrook Mill, one of Richard Arkwright's mills. Turn right and walk along the road to Upperdale.

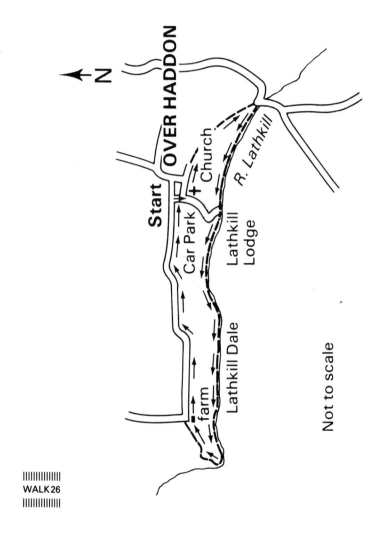

WALK 26

N

Start

OVER HADDON

Church

Car Park

R. Lathkill

Lathkill
Lodge

Lathkill Dale

farm

Not to scale

LATHKILL DALE

WALK 26

★

6 miles (9.5 km)

OS Landranger 119, White Peak

This is a gem of a dale; thickly wooded with a clear running river, most of it a National Nature Reserve. The walk starts at the Over Haddon car park near St Ann's church (SK 203 665).

Take the road at the back of the toilets and walk to the other end of the village, passing the small Wesleyan Reform chapel. At the very end of the street, just past the Lathkill Hotel, pass through a stile in the wall corner and make the descent across the fields. The way is a gradual descent towards the far valley bottom. First cross the field to the stile in the middle of the opposing wall. The next stile is at the bottom corner of the field. Skirt around the wood beyond. Descend more rapidly to join a road and descend this almost to the river bridge.

Turn right on the valley path just before the river bridge and begin the delightful walk up Lathkill Dale. Soon can be seen a series of manmade weirs built for the greater enjoyment of the fishing fraternity. This, of course, is Izaak Walton country. The only building passed is Lathkill Lodge and when reached turn right a little way up the road, but almost at once turn left to rejoin the valley path. The stone pillars met further upstream belong to the mining age. The most important part of lead mining was not collecting the metal itself, but getting rid of the water and this was done with an ingenious series of ducts, or soughs. The stone pillars are the remains of one such system.

When a wooden bridge is reached, where the trees finish on both sides of the valley, take the steps up the hillside to the right and climb above the rocks by a path to the fields above. At the top cross a field to a stile to the right of a gate, then cross to the wood ahead and beyond the wood to the left of a barn to enter a farm yard. Pass through the farm and at the road turn right and walk back to Over Haddon.

GRATTON DALE

WALK 27

★

6 miles (9.5 km)

OS Landranger 119, White Peak

Gratton Dale is largely a dry valley with a stream at the very beginning. There are trees, but the dale is not thickly wooded. The next dale to be entered is Long Dale, practically bereft of trees, a pleasant, rolling dale. Middleton is a delightful village where everything seems old, including the converted houses. The walk starts in Middleton (SK 196 632), where the car may be parked.

Walk along the road south from the village, passing St Michael's church and opposite it a barn-like building with a clock. Take the first left turn, signposted as a cul-de-sac, and walk as far as the stream where a gate crosses the road.

Climb a stile on the left and, after negotiating the marshy ground, climb the hill just to the left of a fence and later a hedge. Further up the hill, keeping to the right of power lines and parallel with them, walk across the fields to join a narrow road descending from the hill above. Turn right and descend by the road to the stream. Walk along the road at the valley bottom until a telephone box is reached at Dale End Farm. Turn right through a stile at the sign 'Public Footpath to Gratton Dale ¾'.

Follow the path along the bottom of the dale until its end. This is where houses can be seen ahead at the top of a rise beyond a gated wall. Pass through the gate then through a gate on the right to enter another valley. This is Long Dale.

Walk along the valley bottom and after passing through a

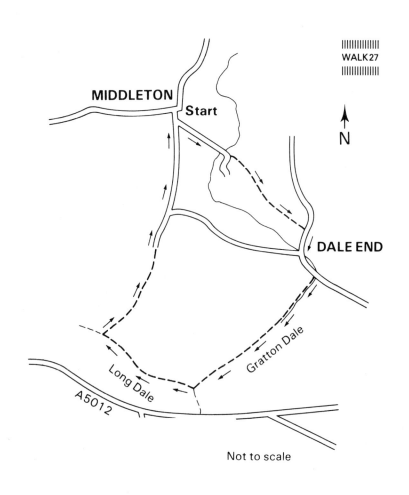

WALK 27

MIDDLETON

Start

N

DALE END

Gratton Dale

Long Dale

A5012

Not to scale

gate barring the way bear right up the hill on a grassed track leaving the valley. At the top of the rise, when the path approaches a wall turn right through a gate in the wall to join a path to the left of a wall. Further along at a barn the path passes to the right of a wall and becomes a track. Lower down, the track passes through a gate and becomes a walled track. When the track joins a road continue in the same direction and walk back to Middleton.

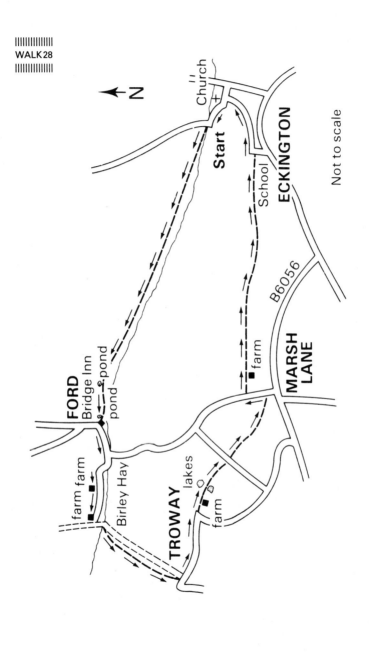

WALK 28

N

Church

Start

ECKINGTON

School

B6056

MARSH LANE

FORD

Bridge Inn

pond

pond

farm

farm farm

Birley Hay

TROWAY

lakes

farm

Not to scale

ECKINGTON
FORD

WALK 28

★

7 miles (11 km)

OS Landranger 110, 119 and 120

Eckington has associations with the Sitwell family and an interesting church, St Peter and Paul, which dates back to the 12th century. The walk starts at the church (SK 432 798). Ford is an attractive village by a stream where there was obviously once a ford.

Walk along Mill Road in a westerly direction and after it crosses a stream turn left on to a track through a wood. When a gate crosses the track take the stile just to the right of the gate and walk along the field edge, at first parallel to the track with its 'Private' notices. Just after the field opens out to give distant views turn left over a stile into a wood. After a short while the path leaves the trees to cross a field and continues by the same wood. Further along the path passes through a stile and into the wood.
   Very soon another path is joined and passes to the left side of a pond. Follow the path into Ford arriving there at the Bridge inn. Prior to the village is the local fishing pond and picnic area. Walk through the village and when the road makes a sharp left bend up Ford Hill take the road to the right indicated as a cul-de-sac. Walk along the lane until the second farm is reached. Prior to the first farm is a lake to the left and beyond the lake an Elizabethan manor house. Not too long ago it was possible to walk by the lake and enjoy the beauty of the scene, but a more recent owner has removed all access

85

to the lake and indeed removed practically all the view as well.

At the second farm turn left at a signpost 'Bridleway to Troway – the Sheffield Way' down a hedge-lined path and after crossing the stream below take the left fork. Start the climb, at first between high hedges, but when possible walk on the field path at the other side of the right hand hedge, keeping parallel to the enclosed path. The path eventually reaches the road at Troway at a farm. Turn left on the road and at the first sharp right bend go forward on the track to Greatfold Farm. Beyond the farm continue on the same track, then on the path beyond a stile to the right of a hedge. At the next stile turn slightly right to descend a field and take the path across the foot of a small lake.

Climb the path on the other side of the lake and, after leaving the wood, ascend a field directly away from the wood. When a track is joined turn left, but after a few yards take a stile on the right to cross a field. At the next stile turn right and walk along the field edge to the next track. Cross it and after climbing another stile climb the hill in the same direction. To the right is a dirt race track. When another track is reached turn right and just before reaching a house climb over a stile, taking a path across to join the road leading to Ford Hill, and emerge on to it to the left of Marsh Lane T junction and its war memorial.

Turn left and after 100 yards turn right on to a track signed 'Public Bridleway, Eckington 1¼'. After passing through a farm take the field path alongside hedges switching hedge sides and generally making a beeline for Eckington church, whose spire can be seen from time to time. Just prior to a large housing estate the path becomes a track and bypasses the estate, eventually entering Eckington at a school. Walk down Stead Street and walk along to return to the church.

HOLMESFIELD
BARLOW

WALK 29

★

6 miles (9.5 km)

OS Landranger 119, White Peak

This is a pleasant, pastoral walk and it could not be otherwise with such delightful names as Brindwoodgate, Cartledge, Unthank, Rose Wood, Rumbling Street, Muckspout Farm and Wilday met along the way. There are also several old manor houses – Cartledge Hall, Unthank Hall and Barlow Woodseats. The walk starts at the northern end of Common Side (SK 336 757), a village a few miles northwest of Chesterfield.

Take the road opposite the sign 'Cutthorpe 2 Chesterfield 4 B6051' one way and 'Killthorpe 1 Hathersage 9 B6051' the other. The narrower road forms part of a small triangle of roads. After about a ¼ mile, at a T junction where the road zigzags, turn left and 30 yards along the road turn right on to a track. A few yards further on take the left bearing path and, on reaching two gates, take the stile between to walk up the field edge keeping parallel to the hedged path. This is a gradual climb of just under a mile. Looking back, as the gentle climb proceeds, it is possible to see Chesterfield's crooked spire.

When the way ahead is blocked by an unstiled hedge, walk to the right alongside the hedge and turn left into a field to walk into Cartledge, which can be seen ahead. Just before reaching Millthorpe Lane, Cartledge Hall can be seen.

At the road, turn left for a few yards then right into a field

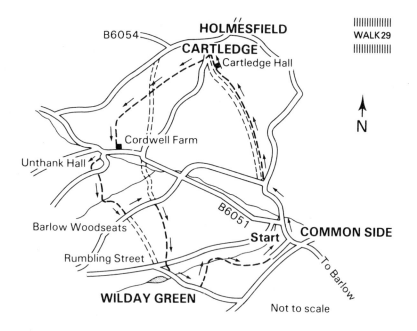

at the sign 'Public Footpath to Unthank 1¼'. The path is fairly clear, gradually bearing left to drop down to Cordwell Farm. Directions, if necessary, are as follows. Walk to the left of a wall and hedge, crossing a small stream and stile at the bottom of the hill. Forward to the far bottom left hand corner of the next field. Stile. Cross the next field to a stone post, to cut the field corner. Walk along the left side of the hedge. Stile. Walk straight across two fields to cross a stream. Follow the field path. Stile. Walk along the top side of the next hedge. Stile. Bear slightly left across the next field. Stile. Head for Cordwell Farm below.

Turn right along the road and take the first left turn on the Unthank Road. After a short walk along it, turn right over a stile next to a gate and along a path next to a hedge. After taking a further stile climb a field towards an old building on the skyline. This is Unthank Hall, now a farm. The path emerges on to a road to the left of the hall.

Turn left into Unthank and just after Yew Tree Cottage turn right into a field at a public footpath signpost at a stile, crossing to a hedge. Walk along the hedge side first on the left, then the right side to enter the wood ahead at a stile. Take a path bearing left to cross a stream, climb the banking at the other side and on through the wood.

After leaving the wood strike across a field aiming for the left of buildings ahead. After crossing a stile take the left side of a hedge, cross a stream and climb the hill to join the road at Barlow Woodseats.

Turn left and walk to the next group of buildings at Johnnygate. Turn right into a field at the sign 'Public Foot-path to Oxtonrakes' keeping to the right of a hedge, passing over a stile into a wood. Take the path to the right in the wood. After the stile leading out of the wood cross a field to a farm on the skyline. At the farm cross the road to another 'Public Footpath' sign next to a small pond and cross the field to join the road seen ahead. Just before the road a stream is crossed and the path bears right on to the road.

Turn left along the road until the house 'Wilday Meadow' is reached. Turn left at the public footpath sign and take the path to Common Side as follows. Walk on the left of a wall. Stile. Cross two fields to a wood edge. Walk at a field edge next to the wood. Stile in the field corner and down through the wood. Stile. Cross the field and stream by the bridge. Turn right to follow the stream and recross it. Climb the hill away from the water and the wood. Cross the fields leading to a housing estate. This is the edge of Common Side and a short walk through the estate takes you back to the starting point.

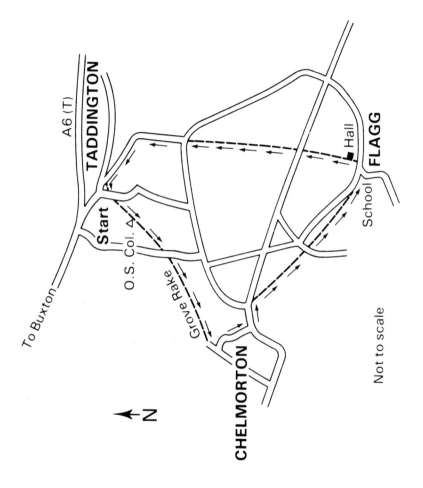

TADDINGTON

A6 (T)

FLAGG

Hall

Start

O.S. Col. △

School

To Buxton

Grove Rake

CHELMORTON

←N

Not to scale

TADDINGTON
CHELMORTON, FLAGG

WALK 30

★

6 miles (9.5 km)

OS Landranger 119, White Peak

These three similar villages could almost be called mountain villages, as Taddington and Chelmorton lie above the 1,000 ft mark and Flagg is almost that. Taddington and Chelmorton possess interesting relics which are worth a visit. All around is evidence of old workings and the villages have strong mining associations. The walk is over agricultural land and wherever one looks there is a tapestry of limestone-walled fields. As a consequence there are many stiles to climb or negotiate, some of which take some finding. Fortunately the routes on this triangular walk are almost in a straight line so that errors in navigation should be fairly easily corrected. The walk starts at the church end of Taddington (SK 140 712), and the car may be left in the village.

Take the Flagg road signposted at the beginning and almost immediately turn right over a stile and pass between the houses into a field. Turn half right up the hill to a stile in a wall and shortly after enter a road. Cross the road and take the path at the sign 'Public Footpath to Chelmorton 2'. Climb the hill diagonally, crossing short fields all the time climbing towards the highest point. After passing three fields in this manner pass through a gap in a wall next to a stake, then up the hill to a few trees. Pass into a field to the right of the trees and across a field to a stile at the far corner.

Beyond the stile is an artificially raised mound with pipes

91

sticking out of the top. In the next field beyond the mound is an Ordnance column, marking, at 1,483 feet, the highest point for miles.

The way now goes along the left side of a wall, over the other side of which is the column, for field after field until shortly after Fivewells Farm lying just to the right. This is at a farm road. Turn right and almost immediately left at the sign 'Public Bridleway, Chelmorton ½'. From the signpost the path is along Grove Rake, a now overgrown, ancient working. Continue to Chelmorton arriving at the village to the right of the church.

At the first road junction turn left and also left at the next junction. Cross the crossroads ahead and after the first field on the right pass through a stile into a field to head for the far corner where the remains of an old wall meet another wall. Bear right to follow this wall to a tree and a stile just ahead. After negotiating the stile bear slightly left eventually reaching the wall ahead. Well before the wall corner, where the wall unaccountably turns right for 3 yards then left again, climb the stile and head across the field towards a large copse to the left of a farm visible ahead. Two-thirds of the way along an opposing wall take a stile in the wall and across the next field to a gateway to the right of the copse. Bear slightly right to enter a road at a footpath signpost.

Directly opposite take a stile into a field to make for a copse ahead. Keeping to its left continue into Flagg to join the road almost at the school. The path from Town Head is practically parallel to the road, so that is where to head for if navigation doubts creep in.

At the crossroads ahead turn left into Flagg Hall Farm drive, passing directly through the farm yard on to an open track beyond, keeping to the left of an old wall and a line of trees. Cross the next field passing a single tree and across the next field to join a road to the left of farm buildings and trees visible from Flagg Hall Farm. Turn right along the road then just before the farm road take a stile into a field on the left to bypass the farm, which seems to double as a briquetting works. When 200 yards past the farm, turn right through a stile and head for another stile diagonally across the field.

The way now is a straight line towards a single building and two trees. When a wall blocks the way, walk beside it to the next gap and then head for the stile near the building.

Cross a very short field then walk up the middle of the next field. Passing over the next stile bear slightly right to the wall corner then cross the next field to join the Flagg–Taddington road. Take the Taddington road and descend to the village.